WRITTEN BY TAYLOR EATON
DESIGNED BY STEPHANIE WICKER-CAMPBELL
EDITED BY BAYLEE FOX

COSMIC WEALTH CODES

MUSE ORACLE PRESS

PUBLISHED BY MUSE ORACLE PRESS PTY LTD

Cosmic Wealth Codes™ Journal

ISBN: 978-1-7635869-1-8

Published by Muse Oracle Press Pty Ltd, 2024.

Cosmic Wealth Codes Journal: Activate and Amplify Abundance in Your Life

Author: Taylor Eaton
Designer: Stephanie Wicker-Campbell
Editor: Baylee Fox

Dear Soul,

Can you feel it? Can you feel the energy of abundance swirling through the space around you? Can you feel it moving within you?

Maybe you can feel it buzzing within your body and soul. Or perhaps it seems distant or even non-existent. Whether you can sense it or not...it's there—around and within you.

Oceans of riches, divinely orchestrated prosperity, and an overflow of material wealth await you, for you are a part of this infinitely expanding universe. You have access to all the endless potential that the cosmos holds for all forms of abundance.

Wealth—in all senses of the word—is your birthright. The truth is that you already have all the tools within you that you need to manifest limitless prosperity into your life.

So, are you ready to learn to leverage them and co-create the wealth you desire with the universe?

It's time to awaken the divine cosmic codes for abundance that reside all around and within you.

With love and abundance,

Taylor

Activate and Amplify
Abundance in Your Life

How to Use This Journal

The prompts and affirmations within these pages have been channeled from the timeless wisdom of the universe—from the Arrow collective (hailing from the Orion constellation), archetypal energies of deities such as Artemis and Hekate, and the all-abundant Source itself.

The words and illustrations alike are uniquely designed to activate the wealth codes you possess and help you wield your innate ability to manifest limitless abundance into your life.

Think of this journal as your personal portal to activate and amplify the wealth frequencies that lie dormant within you. Since this is your personal portal, be sure to use it in whatever way feels best to you. You can go through this journal in order, reflecting on one or more affirmations and prompts per day. You can flip to a random page and trust that you will land on whatever guidance, prompt, card reading, or affirmation you need at that moment. It can become a part of your morning or evening routine, intentional manifestation, or self-reflection practices. And, of course, you are welcome—and even encouraged—to revisit affirmations and prompts many times to unlock deeper levels of truths and abundance within them.

No matter where you are on your journey to wealth, this journal will assist you in manifesting more abundance by uncovering new layers of self-awareness, healing, clarity, and more.

Welcome to these pages—to this sacred space that will help you remember your innate ability to tap into the energy of abundance and translate that energy into any form of prosperity you desire.

Card Spreads for Calling in Cosmic Wealth

While powerful on its own, this journal becomes even more powerful when you use it alongside the Cosmic Wealth Codes Affirmation Deck. The deck contains affirmations that are designed to activate your innate wealth codes. Doing a daily card pull from the deck is a perfect way to align yourself with more abundance and is a beautiful way to close out your journaling session.

As this journal allows you the chance to delve deeper into the core messages of the deck and amplify your wealth codes further, it's only fitting to provide you with four special card spreads you can use to do wealth readings for yourself or others.

The following card spreads are intended to be used with the Cosmic Wealth Codes Affirmation Deck, but you can use other tarot or oracle decks of your choosing. If you want to bring even more depth into your readings for abundance, I highly recommend incorporating The Wealthy Woman Oracle Deck.

You can find both the Cosmic Wealth Codes Affirmation Deck and The Wealthy Woman Oracle Deck by scanning the QR Code below:

To use each card spread, shuffle your deck while envisioning the provided question in your mind. Pull the cards and arrange them per the given spread. Once you've placed all the cards, use the provided interpretation guides. When doing readings with affirmation cards, you will sometimes need to interpret the opposite meaning of a card or solely pay attention to certain words or images that stand out to you from the card to find the message intended for you. As always, trust your inner guidance above all else.

Throughout this journal are pages specifically designed to help you dive deep with a card reading using any of the spreads provided here.

Wealth Code Activation Spread

Use this spread to discover what wealth code is ready to be awakened within you and how to activate it. While shuffling, hold the following question in your mind: "What wealth code am I ready to activate?"

Card 1: The wealth code that is ready to be activated within you.

Card 2: What you need to believe or hear in order to activate it.

Card 3: A message to inspire you to take an aligned action that will activate it.

Wealth Code Amplification Spread

This spread is designed to show you which wealth code you already have activated within you and is now ready to be more powerfully leveraged to manifest more abundance into your life. While shuffling, hold the following question in your mind: "What wealth code am I ready to amplify?"

Card 1: The wealth code that is ready to be amplified within you and more intentionally leveraged.

Card 2: The belief you need to release in order to amplify it (interpret the opposite meaning of the affirmation on this card).

Card 3: The belief you need to more fully embrace in order to amplify it.

Card 4: A message to inspire you to take an aligned action that will allow you to leverage this code intentionally.

Card 5: The signs that the universe will use to show you that you've successfully amplified it (look for specific words or images on this card).

Healing Abundance Blocks Spread

Use this spread to identify and heal any mental, emotional, or energetic blocks you may have that are preventing the abundance you desire from coming to you. While shuffling, hold the following question in your mind: “What do I need to hear to identify and heal whatever may be blocking wealth from reaching me?”

1 2 3

Card 1: Heal your past (interpret the opposite meaning of the affirmation on this card to identify a block that stems from your past, then use the affirmation on this card to create and inspire healing of this block).
Card 2: Heal your present (interpret the opposite meaning of the affirmation on this card to identify a block that is draining most of your energy in the present, then use the affirmation on this card to create and inspire healing of this block).
Card 3: The affirmation or message you can repeat to project healing and wholeness into your future.

Aligned Action for Abundance Spread

This spread is designed to help you connect with the universe and receive guidance on what aligned actions you can take to manifest more abundance into your life. While shuffling, hold the following question in your mind: "What is the next step for me to take to call more prosperity into my life?"

Card 1: A message to inspire what action you can take next to call in more wealth.

Card 2: What you need to release in order to successfully do the inspired action (interpret the opposite meaning of the affirmation on this card).

Card 3: What you need to embrace in order to do the inspired action.

Card 4: What you need to keep in mind or look for as you do the inspired action.

Deck Title: Date:

Setting Intentions:

Card Spread:

Cards Pulled:

Interpretation:

Deck Title: Date:

Setting Intentions:

Card Spread:

Cards Pulled:

Interpretation:

Deck Title: Date:

Setting Intentions:

Card Spread:

Cards Pulled:

Interpretation:

Deck Title: Date:

Setting Intentions:

Card Spread:

Cards Pulled:

Interpretation:

My energy is the
currency of the
cosmos.

What area of my life can I direct my conscious attention to today to strengthen my sense of security and abundance?

I am a truly blessed being. What are all the miraculous ways (big or small) wealth has come to me throughout my life?

What bold action have I wanted to take concerning wealth (career, finances, etc.)? How can I take one small step toward it today?

I find it easiest to connect to my higher self/the universe/Source/God when I...

The more I remember my connection to the divine, the more easily money flows to me.

How can I infuse more love into my actions today to attract more abundance?

In what ways am I closing myself off to receiving abundance (in any form it may take)?

What signs do I want the universe to use to show me that abundance is coming my way?

I AM A
COSMIC
MIRACLE
WORTHY OF
INFINITE
WEALTH.

What signs or synchronicities have I seen recently that show me the wealth I desire is coming to me?

If I genuinely believed that abundance was my divine birthright, I would...

If I gave myself permission to fully relax today, I would...

I AM THE CREATOR OF
MY WEALTH AND THE
RECEIVER OF IT.

What am I excited to do right now (whether it's seemingly related to money or not)?

I am so grateful that I currently have an abundance of...

What comes easily to me? How are each of these things valuable (to myself, others, or the world)?

If I tune into my intuition, I can hear it is saying that to manifest more wealth into my life, I need to...

What are all the ways that abundance has come to me in the last several days?

Wealth is woven
into my DNA like
stars woven into the
tapestry of the sky.

Deck Title:

Date:

Setting Intentions:

Card Spread:

Cards Pulled:

Interpretation:

Deck Title: Date:

Setting Intentions:

Card Spread:

Cards Pulled:

Interpretation:

Deck Title: Date:

Setting Intentions:

Card Spread:

Cards Pulled:

Interpretation:

Deck Title: Date:

Setting Intentions:

Card Spread:

Cards Pulled:

Interpretation:

What do I now choose to believe in order to allow myself to feel secure whenever abundance appears to flow out of my life faster than it is flowing in?

I realize that I am meant to have an overflow of riches because I already have an overflow of...

Should I work on creating wealth or be more open (and expect) to receive it? Why do I feel pulled in this direction?

How do I feel called to give to others today? What can I contribute that is easy and feels good to give?

By having more abundance, the people around me will benefit because...

What energy am I currently sending out into the universe?

Is it congruent with the wealth I wish to attract?

If not, what is one thing I can do to shift my energy today?

I AM OPEN TO RECEIVING
THE BOUNDLESS WEALTH
OF THE COSMOS.

What beliefs, stories, or habits do I need to release and/or embrace to believe I am innately worthy of all the abundance I desire?

What past experiences do I have that show me that things are actually working out in my favor even when it doesn't look like it?

What fears do I need to release to create space for more abundance in my life?

In this moment, I can release all worries and fears regarding wealth because...

If I knew the wealth I wanted was guaranteed to come to me, I would...

What do I know I need to release to be more authentic to who I am?

How could any challenges I currently face around wealth be happening for me?

I WELCOME THE LESSONS
THE UNIVERSE OFFERS ME
SO THAT I MAY CALIBRATE
TO GREATER SUCCESS.

Deck Title: Date:

Setting Intentions:

Card Spread:

Cards Pulled:

Interpretation:

Deck Title: Date:

Setting Intentions:

Card Spread:

Cards Pulled:

Interpretation:

Deck Title: Date:

Setting Intentions:

Card Spread:

Cards Pulled:

Interpretation:

Deck Title: Date:

Setting Intentions:

Card Spread:

Cards Pulled:

Interpretation:

What is most likely to happen for me where prosperity is concerned?

How do my relationships with other people reflect my current relationship with wealth?

What do I want to change in my relationships with others in order to better reflect my desired relationship with wealth?

What does being "blessed" and "destined for wealth" mean to me? What evidence do I have to support that I am blessed and destined for wealth according to my own definitions?

If I already had the wealth I desire, what would I think, say, feel, or do differently?

What do I want to start to believe is most likely to happen for me where prosperity is concerned?

I am more prosperous today than I was yesterday because...

What does “abundance” mean to me?

My inner sense of
wealth is the universe's
blueprint for my
external experience.

In my heart and soul, I know wealth is...

What will I do with the wealth that the universe brings me?

I am a conduit for
the universe's riches.

Thinking that the wealth I desire is inevitable makes me feel...

What immeasurable or intangible forms of abundance do I already possess?

THE UNIVERSE SPEAKS
THROUGH MY INTUITION,
GUIDING ME TO THE
ABUNDANCE I DESIRE.

How can I imagine wealth coming to me today (in big, small, expected, and unexpected) ways?

What am I currently holding onto that is dampening my natural ability to feel abundant?

What am I afraid of happening if I were to suddenly receive everything I desire?

Having more abundance will help me become the best version of myself in the following ways...

When I think about wealth as something carried in my soul that extends beyond this moment in time, I...

What lesson can I learn from any current challenges I am experiencing around wealth? What opportunities for growth are available to me here?

I AM A CHILD OF THE
COSMOS. ABUNDANCE IS
MY DIVINE BIRTHRIGHT.

Deck Title: Date:

Setting Intentions:

Card Spread:

Cards Pulled:

Interpretation:

Deck Title: Date:

Setting Intentions:

Card Spread:

Cards Pulled:

Interpretation:

Deck Title:

Date:

Setting Intentions:

Card Spread:

Cards Pulled:

Interpretation:

Deck Title:

Date:

Setting Intentions:

Card Spread:

Cards Pulled:

Interpretation:

The things that make me feel wealthy are...

What blessings have I recently received from the universe?

I feel that the universe is guiding me toward abundance by...

What support do I have available to me (from others, myself, the universe, etc.) on my wealth journey?

How can I create more opportunities for money to come to me?

What does my life look like in my wildest, wealthiest dreams?

I now ask the universe to provide me with the resources, strength, and courage to heal the things blocking me from the wealth I desire, including...

Every cell of my being
naturally vibrates at
the frequency of
inevitable wealth.

What activities help me relax (mentally and physically) so that I can receive ideas, inspiration, and energy to manifest more wealth?

What support do I have available to me (from others, myself, the universe, etc.) on my wealth journey?

I feel that the universe is guiding me toward abundance by...

What can I do right now to feel wealthy?

Today, I will take time to truly cherish and enjoy...

I AM THE ARCHITECT OF
MY FORTUNES, AND THE
UNIVERSE IS THE BUILDER.

Today, I choose to celebrate this life and all the prosperity it contains by...

How does my perspective around wealth shift when I think about being a part of this infinitely abundant universe?

I AM DIVINELY DESIGNED
TO BE THE UNIVERSE'S
VESSEL FOR WEALTH.

About the Author

Taylor Eaton is a renowned wealth activator dedicated to channeling guidance on all aspects of abundance. Her influential works, including the Cosmic Wealth Codes Affirmation Deck, The Wealthy Woman Oracle Deck, and The Way of the Wealthy Woman Journal, weave a tapestry of wisdom to empower individuals to transform their financial realities and inspire a global paradigm shift around money.

As a revered oracle deck creator, entrepreneur, and business mentor, Taylor's unique spiritual money tools have impacted the lives of thousands by reshaping their financial landscapes and healing their spirits. Her distinctive approach seamlessly integrates mindset work, meditation, Human Design, magick, channeling, and oracle card readings, offering holistic and personalized strategies tailored to each individual's wealth journey. Taylor's philosophy is firmly rooted in the belief that everyone possesses the innate ability to create a life of boundless abundance and deserves access to the spiritual tools required to manifest it.

From gardening to channeling sacred writings, Taylor delights in getting lost in the enchanting tranquility of nature and the simple pleasures of life. She often seeks solace hiking through the lush forests of the Pacific Northwest, accompanied by her husband, daughter, and their dogs.

Learn more about Taylor, her other works, ways to connect with her, and exclusive gifts for abundance by scanning the QR code below.

About the Artist

Stephanie Wicker-Campbell is an intuitive illustrator driven by the essence of the soul, unraveling the enchantment within the ordinary. Born in the United States, she currently resides in Sydney. Stephanie's passion for travel and adventure is just one of the many sources from which she draws her artistic inspiration.

Stephanie's work covers a broad spectrum and channels a diverse array of palettes, making her a sought-after partner for published projects. Found on oracle decks, journals, and book covers, her spellbinding designs resonate with audiences worldwide.